TEENY WITCH
and
The Terrible
TWINS

by LIZ MATTHEWS
illustrated by CAROLYN LOH

Troll Associates

Library of Congress Cataloging-in-Publication Data

Matthews, Liz.
   Teeny Witch and the terrible twins / by Liz Matthews; illustrated
by Carolyn Loh.
      p.   cm.
   Summary: Teeny Witch's attempt to watch her aunts' house and
babysit some terrible twins at the same time results in horrible
chaos, but her aunts have a surprising reaction.
   ISBN 0-8167-2266-8 (lib. bdg.)   ISBN 0-8167-2267-6 (pbk.)
   [1. Babysitters—Fiction.   2. Twins—Fiction.   3. Aunts—Fiction.
4. Witches—Fiction.]   I. Loh, Carolyn, ill.   II. Title.
PZ7.M4337Te   1991
[E]—dc20   90-11139

Teeny Witch lived in a large, old house with her three aunts. Teeny loved her aunts very much. But all her aunts were a little strange.

Teeny's Aunt Icky liked to mix up smelly brews in the kitchen. Teeny Witch had to hold her nose whenever Aunt Icky cooked.

Her Aunt Ticky liked making all kinds of weird things. Teeny's house was filled with odd tables, and funny chairs and clocks.

Worst of all was
Teeny's Aunt Vicky.
Aunt Vicky liked to
catch hairy spiders
for her ugly bug
collection.

Teeny Witch wasn't like her aunts. She liked pretty flowers and bright sunshine. She liked parties and playing with friends. Most of all, she liked to go to Moonbeam Mall. Moonbeam Mall was a fun place to visit.

"Teeny Witch," Aunt Icky called one day. "We're going shopping."

"Watch the house carefully while we're gone," said Aunt Vicky.
"Do a good job and we'll take you to Moonbeam Mall when we return," said Aunt Icky.

When her aunts were gone, Teeny Witch looked
around the house. There wasn't a single thing out of
place. The kitchen smelled clean. Even the jars
containing Aunt Vicky's bug collection were in a neat
row on the mantel.

"This will be easy," Teeny Witch said. She plopped down in a chair.

Just then the telephone rang.

"Hello. Teeny Witch speaking," said Teeny.
"Hello, Teeny. This is Mrs. McNaughty," said the
caller. "Can you baby-sit my twins, Henry and Harriet?"

Teeny Witch thought about the job. Baby-sitting would give her extra money to spend at the mall. Then she remembered what her aunts had said about watching the house.

"I am sorry," Teeny Witch replied. "I would like to baby-sit. But I cannot leave my house."

"I will bring the twins to your house," Mrs. McNaughty answered. "You can watch them there."

What a great idea! thought Teeny Witch. What an
easy way to make extra spending money!
    "Okay, Mrs. McNaughty," Teeny Witch replied.
"Bring the twins right over."

Minutes later
the doorbell rang.

Teeny Witch opened the door. There stood
Mrs. McNaughty and her twins.
"Hello, Henry. Hello, Harriet," said Teeny Witch.
Henry and Harriet didn't answer. They just smiled.

"I will hurry back," Mrs.
McNaughty promised.

As soon as her back was turned,
Henry and Harriet dashed into
the house.

16

Teeny Witch turned around. "Oh no!" she cried. Henry McNaughty was bouncing on the new couch.

Harriet McNaughty was jumping on Aunt Ticky's favorite chair.

Boing! Boing! Boing!

Sprong! Sprong! Sprong! went the springs of the couch.
Squeak! Squeak! Squeak! went the chair.
"What terrible twins these McNaughtys are!"
cried Teeny.

"Stop bouncing and jumping!" Teeny Witch ordered. "Stop right now!"

Henry and Harriet stopped. But they didn't stop soon enough. The new couch was now all lumpy and bumpy.

"Oh no," groaned Teeny Witch. "Aunt Ticky will be so angry when she sees this. Why did I ever agree to baby-sit?"

Teeny Witch looked at the terrible twins. "Well,
what do you have to say?" she asked them.
"WE'RE HUNGRY!" Henry shouted.
"We want cookies to eat!" Harriet hollered.
"I'm sorry, but we're out of cookies,"
Teeny Witch replied.
"WAH!" cried the McNaughty twins very loudly.
"WAH! WAH! WE WANT COOKIES!"

Teeny Witch covered her ears.

"Okay! Okay!" she said. "I will bake cookies. But stop crying!"

The twins stopped howling and smiled.

"We'll help," they shouted.

In the kitchen, Teeny took out a big mixing bowl. "What kind of cookies should I make?" she asked the twins.

"Kookie cookies," said the twins.

"How do you make kookie cookies?" Teeny Witch asked.

"We'll show you," the twins answered. They got the things they needed for their special cookies.

Harriet dumped flour into the bowl.
"Now for milk," Henry said.
"That milk smells funny," sniffed Harriet.
"It's sour milk," said Teeny Witch. "My aunt uses it for her special brews."
"It's perfect," Henry snickered. And he poured it into the bowl.

The twins found other things they needed on Aunt Icky's spice shelf.
They put in crushed garlic.
They put in chopped onions . . . and a little bit of glop.

"It's not finished yet," Harriet said. "We need some rotten eggs."

"Here they come!" Henry shouted as he opened the refrigerator door.

"Wait!" called Teeny Witch. "Those are Aunt Icky's special eggs."

But Henry didn't wait. He took out two eggs and tossed them to Harriet.

Splat! Splat! The eggs hit the floor.

"I need more eggs," Harriet shouted. "Throw some more."

27

"Oh no you don't!" Teeny Witch yelled.

"WAH! Without rotten eggs we can't make kookie cookies," Harriet cried. "WAH! WAH! WAH!"

"Here!" said Teeny Witch as she handed Harriet two rotten eggs. "Now, please be quiet!"

Harriet smiled an impish smile and took the eggs.

The terrible twins laughed and mixed the eggs into the dough.

Teeny Witch grumbled and cleaned the egg mess off the floor.

The floor smelled bad.

The cookie dough smelled worse.

Phew! The whole kitchen smelled icky.

"Yuck! I'm not hungry anymore," Henry said.

"Me either," said Harriet.

"Aren't you going to bake your kookie cookies?" asked Teeny Witch. "Aren't you going to eat them?"

"Eat kookie cookies?" laughed Henry. "Never!"

"Kookie cookies are fun to make," said Harriet. "But they're not fun to eat."

"Oh no," groaned Teeny Witch.

There's No ×× Place Like ×× Home

Teeny Witch cleaned up the kitchen. Her magic broom helped. Soon the kitchen looked clean. But it didn't smell clean.

"What can happen next?" thought Teeny Witch.

Harriet pointed at Teeny's broom. "Is that broom really magic?" she asked.

"Does it fly?" asked Henry.

"Yes," replied Teeny Witch. "It really is a magic broom that flies. But don't be afraid of it."

The twins looked at each other. They smiled. "We're not afraid of the broom," said Henry.

"We want to play with it," Harriet said. "Let's play tag."

Quick as a wink the twins jumped on the broom.
ZOOM! Into the living room the terrible twins flew.
"Tag! You're it!" yelled Harriet to Teeny. "Catch us
if you can."

"Come back here!" Teeny Witch shouted. She chased after the twins.

Zoom! Zoom! Around and around the living room the nasty McNaughty twins soared.

"Be careful!" Teeny Witch cried as the twins whizzed by the mantel. "Watch out for those jars!" On the mantel was Aunt Vicky's ugly bug collection.

One by one the jars toppled off the mantel. Their lids
popped off. Ugly bugs crawled, climbed, and crept away.
There were ugly bugs here, there, and everywhere.

"Yikes!" yelled Teeny Witch. "You let Aunt Vicky's bugs loose! Come down here at once, you terrible McNaughty twins!"

The tone of Teeny Witch's voice made the twins gulp. They landed on the lumpy bumpy couch. And for the first time all day, they sat quiet and still.

Just then the doorbell rang. It was Mr. and Mrs. McNaughty.

"I told you I wouldn't be long," Mrs. McNaughty said.

Mrs. McNaughty looked at Henry and Harriet sitting
quietly on the couch.

"I can see my darling twins were good as usual,"
she said.

Mr. McNaughty looked at Teeny and smiled, as if he
knew the truth. Then he winked at Teeny and paid her.

"Let's go, children," Mrs. McNaughty called.
Zoom! Zip! The terrible twins dashed past Teeny.
  "Goodbye," said Teeny as she watched the
McNaughtys leave. She was very happy to see them go.

Teeny looked the other way. Her three aunts were
coming down the street.

"Oh no," Teeny said. "The furniture looks awful.
The kitchen smells icky. And ugly bugs are everywhere!
What a mess!" she sighed. "I'll never get to go to
the mall now."

Aunt Ticky, Aunt Vicky, and Aunt Icky came up the walk.

"Hello, Teeny," said Aunt Ticky.

"Did you watch the house?" asked Aunt Vicky.

"Did you do a good job?" Aunt Icky asked.

"I watched the house as well as I could," said Teeny Witch. "And I baby-sat the McNaughty twins, too. It was not an easy thing to do."

Teeny's three aunts nodded and went into the house.

"My furniture!" cried Aunt Ticky. "My furniture looks really weird! It's lumpy! It's bumpy! It's bent out of shape! I love it!"

"My kitchen!" yelled Aunt Icky. "It smells really icky. How wonderful! What a nice smell to come home to!"

Teeny Witch couldn't believe her ears. Her aunts weren't angry at all. Then she heard Aunt Vicky call her.

"Teeny Witch, come here," Aunt Vicky said.

Teeny Witch gulped and went inside.

"Where are my ugly bugs?" Aunt Vicky asked.

"They got out," Teeny Witch said. "They are all over the house."

"Great!" cried Aunt Vicky. "Now I can have fun catching them all over again. What a nice thing to do. Thank you, Teeny."

Teeny Witch smiled. Her three witch aunts really were very strange. But that made her love them even more.

"Let's all go to Moonbeam Mall," Aunt Icky said to Teeny Witch.

"Oh boy!" Teeny shouted.

Teeny and her aunts climbed into their car. And thanks to baby-sitting, Teeny Witch had lots of extra money to spend at the mall.